LIZARDS AT LARGE

21 Remarkable Reptiles at Their Actual Size

ROXIE MUNRO

COLLARED LIZARD

HOLIDAY HOUSE • NEW YORK

To Vicki Cobb, science writer extraordinaire

FENCE LIZARD

Text and illustrations copyright © 2023 by Roxie Munro

All Rights Reserved

HOLIDAY HOUSE is registered in the U.S. Patent and Trademark Office.

Printed and bound in February 2024 at Leo Paper, Heshan, China.

The artwork was created with India ink and colored acrylic inks on 100% cotton rag paper.

www.holidayhouse.com

First Paperback Edition

3 5 7 9 10 8 6 4 2

Library of Congress Cataloging-in-Publication Data

Names: Munro, Roxie, author, illustrator.

Title: Lizards at large : 21 remarkable reptiles at their actual size / Roxie Munro.

Description: First edition. | New York : Holiday House, [2023] | Audience:

Ages 4–8 | Audience: Grades K–1 | Summary: "True-to-size illustrations

of lizards from habitats around the world accompany simple, informative

text that introduces their amazing abilities"—Provided by publisher.

Identifiers: LCCN 2022052506 | ISBN 9780823453603 (hardcover)

Subjects: LCSH: Lizards—Juvenile literature. | Lizards—Size—Juvenile literature.

Classification: LCC QL666.L2 M84 2023 | DDC 597.9514/1—dc23/eng/20221229

LC record available at https://lccn.loc.gov/2022052506

ISBN: 978-0-8234-5360-3 (hardcover)

ISBN: 978-0-8234-5879-0 (paperback)

INTRODUCTION

MADAGASCAR
DAY LIZARD

Since the beginning of recorded history, human beings have been fascinated by lizards. Lizard motifs are found throughout the world—from China to Turkey, from Italy to Scandinavia, and from Australia to the Americas. They have been called serpents, dragons, devils, monsters, and dinosaurs. Lizards appear in mythology, religious and other texts, decoration, architecture, and art.

All lizards are reptiles, but all reptiles are not lizards. Reptiles also include tortoises, turtles, snakes, and crocodilians. Lizards are scaly-skinned reptiles that are usually distinguished from snakes because they have legs (except in the case of worm lizards). Most have movable eyelids (while a snake's eyes are always open). Unlike snakes, lizards have external ear openings. Most snakes have one long, skinny lung, but lizards have two.

Lizards are *cold-blooded*, unlike people, who are warm-blooded. While we generate heat ourselves internally by burning the food we eat, lizards use external sources. To heat their bodies, they may lie in the sun, or to cool them, they may lie in the shade or go underground.

Lizards should also not be confused with amphibians, such as frogs or salamanders, which can look like lizards. Amphibians are not reptiles either, although they are cold-blooded. Unlike lizards, who have lungs and live mainly on land, amphibians live in the water (breathing through gills) as well as on land (breathing with lungs). Amphibians have smooth, moist skin, in contrast to the dry scales of lizards. They lay soft, jellylike eggs that morph into adults later, while most reptiles lay leathery or hard-shelled eggs. When reptiles are born, they are smaller versions of adults.

There are about 6,000 *species* of lizards, living in forests, deserts, and tropical areas all over the world. There are far more kinds of lizards than all the other kinds of reptiles combined, from a tiny .5-inch (1.3-centimeter) nano-chameleon to the 10-foot (3-meter) Komodo dragon. They have lots of different behaviors, habits, diets, colors, sizes, patterns, defenses, and mating rituals.

Most of the time, a lizard's flexible, lithe body moves by bending and twisting, to crawl, jump, swim, run, climb, or even glide. They use their tails to maintain balance. Their legs and feet are specialized, as we will see—some can even walk upside down on glass. The shape of lizards' tongues varies, from fleshy, fat, pink tongues to slender, forked tongues. Some even have blue tongues. Many have large eyes with slit-like pupils, but a few have small eyes, which are better for keeping out sand.

Lizards defend themselves in some incredible ways. Some lizards change color, or *camouflage*, and wedge or inflate their body into a crevice so a *predator* can't pull them out. They might try to look larger by puffing up with air, expanding a neck frill, or doing push-ups. Or they might try opening a brightly colored mouth extra wide; hissing; exhibiting sharp spines, horns, claws, or bony plates; curling up into a ball; squirting blood from their eyes; or expelling smelly goo. Some can discard their tails, which have detachable bones and come off when grabbed.

Almost all lizards are harmless, and many are helpful. They control pesky bugs and ants; research into their clinging feet has led to new types of bandages; and their *venom* may help scientists understand blood clotting and develop new drugs to help us. Only Gila monsters, Mexican beaded lizards, some iguanas, and a few monitors (including the Komodo dragon) have venomous bites, and their venoms are usually not as strong as those of snakes.

There are several main types of lizards. Small lizards called geckos live on every continent except Antarctica. Monitors, including Komodo dragons, have long bodies, can run fast, and live in grasslands, rainforests, and deserts in Africa, Asia, and Australia. Iguanas can also be big—up to six feet (1.8 meters) long—and live in the Americas. They're omnivorous and among the most colorful and dramatic lizards.

Lizards have been around much longer than even the dinosaurs—they go back more than 300,000,000 years. Lizards have been at large for an incredibly long time.

LINED LEAF-TAILED GECKO

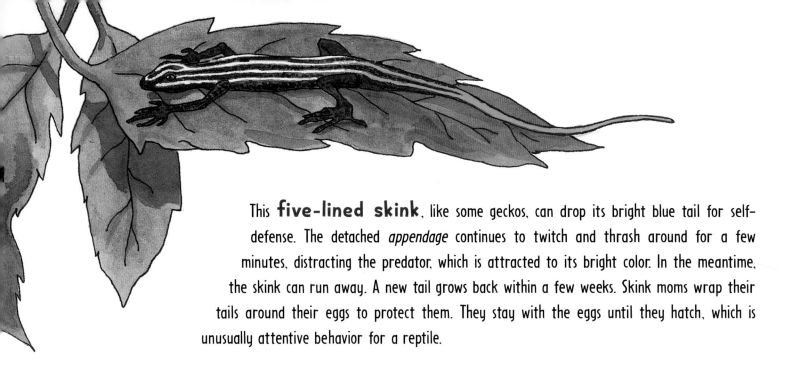

This **five-lined skink**, like some geckos, can drop its bright blue tail for self-defense. The detached *appendage* continues to twitch and thrash around for a few minutes, distracting the predator, which is attracted to its bright color. In the meantime, the skink can run away. A new tail grows back within a few weeks. Skink moms wrap their tails around their eggs to protect them. They stay with the eggs until they hatch, which is unusually attentive behavior for a reptile.

The **armadillo girdled lizard** looks like a tiny dragon. It has a fascinating defense against predators. It rolls into a ball and grasps its tail, which is covered with rings of sharp spines, in its jaw. That creates a spiky "fence" or "stockade" around its soft tummy, protecting it. Unlike most lizards, who are solitary creatures, it lives in social groups from four to six up to as many as sixty individuals. It's one of the few lizards that doesn't lay eggs. Females give birth to one or two live young a year.

Despite its spiky features, the **Texas horned lizard** is preyed upon by lots of animals, including hawks, roadrunners, snakes, dogs, coyotes, and larger lizards. But it has developed special defenses.

It can inflate its body up to twice its size, so it looks like a spiny balloon. But the strangest fact about this little lizard is that it can shoot blood from its eyes. The blood squirts from ducts in the corners of its eyes and can travel three to five feet (about 1 to 1.5 meters). It's meant to confuse threatening creatures, but also contains a chemical that is foul-tasting and noxious to dogs, coyotes, and other predators.

Green anoles are famous for acting up. They bob their heads vigorously when they're ready to fight, to establish their territory, or to get the attention of a mate. They display bright *dewlaps* (loose skin under their necks) to warn other males or attract a female. They can instantly change color from brown (when they're calm or sleepy) to green (when they're exerting themselves or feeling threatened) and back again.

The **fringe-toed lizard** switches its legs back and forth like a dancer doing a two-step. It will lift one front leg and the opposite back leg up off the hot ground to cool off. It usually lives in deserts. The "fringe" of scales along its legs and feet acts like snowshoes and keeps it from sinking into the sand. This lizard can run really fast—up to 23 miles per hour (37 kilometers per hour). In the cold of winter, it sometimes tunnels underground in burrows, where it is also protected against predators.

The small leaf-tailed gecko camouflages itself by lying on a tree branch and blending in with the foliage. It has skin the same color and texture as leaves and bark. Some leaf-tailed geckos look like lichen or moss. They flatten against the surface of a tree, with their big, wide tails that match the nearby leaves. If disturbed, this gecko opens its jaws wide, showing a bright red mouth, and emits a loud distress call that resembles a child's scream.

Like the fringe-toed lizard, the sandfish skink lives in deserts and spends most of its time in sand, a shallow inch or so deep, to escape high daytime temperatures. It burrows down using its flat head with a long cone-shaped snout. It has broad toes to help it "swim" in the sand. It can close its small eyes and tiny nostrils to keep out sand. With its legs tucked close to its body, it makes winding movements and can breathe while totally submerged. It inhales oxygen from the little areas of air between the sand particles and sneezes out any sand that gets in its nose or lungs.

As with most geckos, this colorful **gold-dust day gecko's** eyes don't close. Their pupils are wide and round at night, when they are looking for insects. During the day, their pupils are vertical slits. They clean their large eyes with their tongues. Also like many geckos, they have adhesive toe and nail pads with thousands of clingy hairs or tiny bristles that adhere to surfaces. They can walk straight up anything vertical, even glass.

The Florida **worm lizard** is legless. It looks like a blunt, pinkish-colored snake, although some worm lizard species have little bumps where legs used to be on their reptile ancestors many thousands of years ago. They have cylinder-shaped bodies. Their heads are reinforced with extra hard scales that strengthen them for digging and forcing their way through the soil. Worm lizards spend most of their lives underground, except when flooded out by heavy rains. Then, people sometimes discover them on roads or paths and mistake them for extra-big earthworms.

Cute **leopard geckos** are different from other geckos in several ways. Their toes do not have adhesive toe pads, so they can't climb smooth vertical walls. But they can raise themselves up on more or less straight legs above the ground. And unlike most other kinds of geckos, they have movable eyelids and are sometimes said to wink. Like some fish and crocodiles, they are *polyphyodonts*—each of their 100 teeth gets replaced every three or four months.

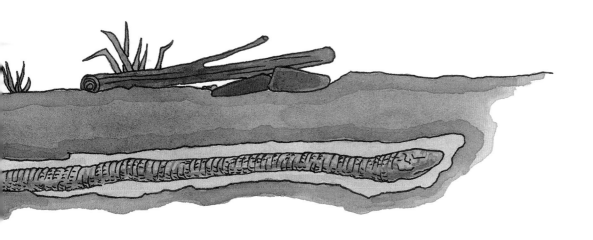

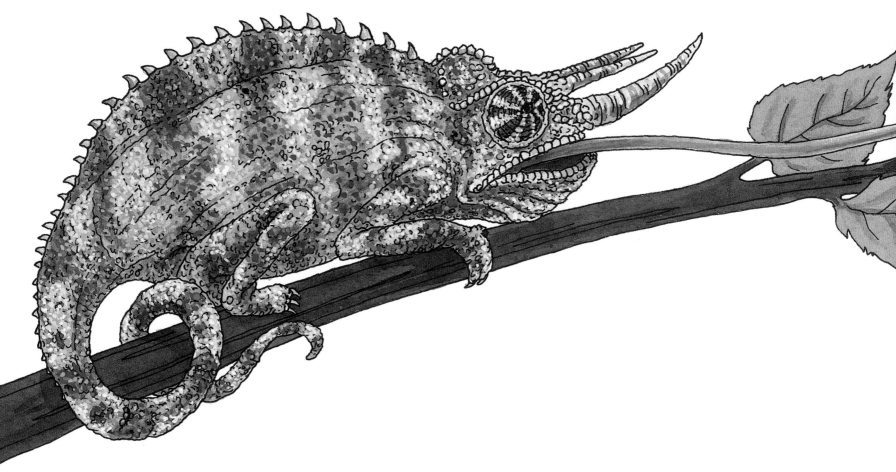

Jackson's chameleons are unique because the males have three horns. Like other chameleons, their tongues can be more than twice as long as their bodies—that would be like a human having a tongue that was 10 feet (3 meters) long! A powerful muscle shoots the tongue out suddenly. The tongue is sticky with saliva and has suction cups on the end to grab dinner, usually bugs, which is pulled back into the mouth. Chameleons also have muscular, prehensile tails, like monkeys. They can pull themselves onto a branch using only their tail.

The wild-looking **thorny devil** has adapted in odd ways to the hot, dry Australian deserts where it lives. When threatened, it buries its head in the sand and raises its tail, which makes it look like a scrubby desert plant. It also has a false "head" attached to the back of its neck. It puts its real head down, which raises the false head to intimidate predators. It has a unique hydration system—drops of dew or rainwater collect in the channels or grooves on its back and drain toward its mouth. It loves ants! Devils will find a trail of ants and eat up to 2,500 in a single meal.

This **parachute gecko** (also called a "flying gecko") spreads wing-like *membranes* on the sides of its body and legs and floats or glides through the air. The flaps help it generate lift, like an airplane taking off. Its broad tail and the webbing between its toes slow its descent. It can glide up to 200 feet (60 meters) and makes a graceful swoop when coming in for a landing.

It can't fly, but the **collared lizard** is one of the few lizards that can run using only its hind legs (making it a *bipedal* animal, like a human). It is really fast and can run up to 17 miles per hour (27 kilometers per hour) to escape predators! Another trick to make itself look bigger and more threatening to rivals is to do push-ups. It lives mainly in the American Western states (and parts of Mexico) in deserts, grasslands, and dry rocky areas.

Like other chameleons, this **veiled chameleon** has protruding eyes. Each eye operates independently of the other. One can be looking at a predator coming, and the other eye can check out a bug for dinner at the same time. Their eyes can look in two different directions at once! Chameleons are also famous for changing colors in seconds, because of their mood, to camouflage themselves, or to attract a mate. They have fused toes, like mittens. There are three on one side of the foot and two on the other. This makes walking on the ground awkward but helps them navigate on the limbs of the trees where they live.

The big-eyed **tokay gecko** has a wide mouth that makes it look like it's smiling. However, its strong jaw has a painful bite. Its name comes from the loud croak it makes, like "token," "tuck-too," "gekk-gekk," or "poo-kay." Sometimes if it's mad or threatened, it chirps, barks, or hisses. It's big for a gecko and has a particularly strong grip with special adhesive foot pads that have thousands of tiny hair-like structures called "setae." Each foot can cling with the strength of up to twenty times the tokay's weight. With just one toe, they can hold on to a vertical surface like a superhero! Scientists are not sure how they do it. Even if the gecko dies, its feet stay strongly attached to the wall.

The **green plumed basilisk** runs really fast on water—up to 7 miles per hour (11.3 kilometers per hour). It has a unique way of slapping its feet, which have special scales on their bottoms, allowing it to skim over the surface. That would be like a human running 100 miles per hour (160 kilometers per hour) with rubber flippers on! It uses its strong back legs, pumps its shorter forelegs, and swings its tail to maintain balance. When the basilisk slows down, it drops to all fours and swims the rest of the way to land. However, if necessary, it can stay submerged underwater for up to ten minutes.

The **Australian frilled lizard** has a ruffled collar that is usually folded around its neck. The collar is supported by spines of *cartilage* (like in our noses and ears) that are attached to its jawbones. To look big and scary and startle predators, it stands on its hind legs, opens its mouth wide (which causes the frill to extend), and loudly hisses. This colorful lizard often walks on two feet, like a human. It lives mainly in trees and woodlands, on a diet of insects. Its favorite foods are butterflies, moths, and their larvae.

The **Gila monster** is the rare lizard with venom. It is slow-moving but can suddenly twist and lock its powerful jaws onto prey, holding on for minutes. Paralyzing venom from glands in its head seeps along grooves in its teeth into the victim. It eats small creatures such as rabbits, mice, birds and their eggs, lizards, snakes, and frogs. It stores extra fat in its chubby tail. Gila monsters may look awkward, but they are agile enough to climb straight up a tree.

Though they might look like scary predators, **green iguanas** are mainly vegetarians. They eat fruit, flowers, and greens. Their favorite place to rest is on a tree branch up in the rainforest canopy or hanging out over the water. Agile climbers, they can also fall down from 50 feet (15 meters) and land unhurt. Iguanas are good swimmers too, propelling themselves through the water with powerful tail strokes instead of using their legs. The dewlap (the loose flap of skin under its neck) regulates its body temperature and can be used to show off in courtship or to establish its territory.

The **Komodo dragon** is the world's largest lizard. It grows up to 10 feet long (3 meters). It has poor vision and hearing and uses its excellent sense of smell as its main food detector. Its forked tongue "samples" the air, processing the scent through specialized organs on the roof of its mouth. It's a *carnivore* with a vicious, venomous bite that can eat prey the size of a goat, deer, or even a water buffalo. But it has a very slow *metabolism*, and can survive on as little as twelve meals a year. Very few people see them because they live on only a few islands in Indonesia in the south Pacific.

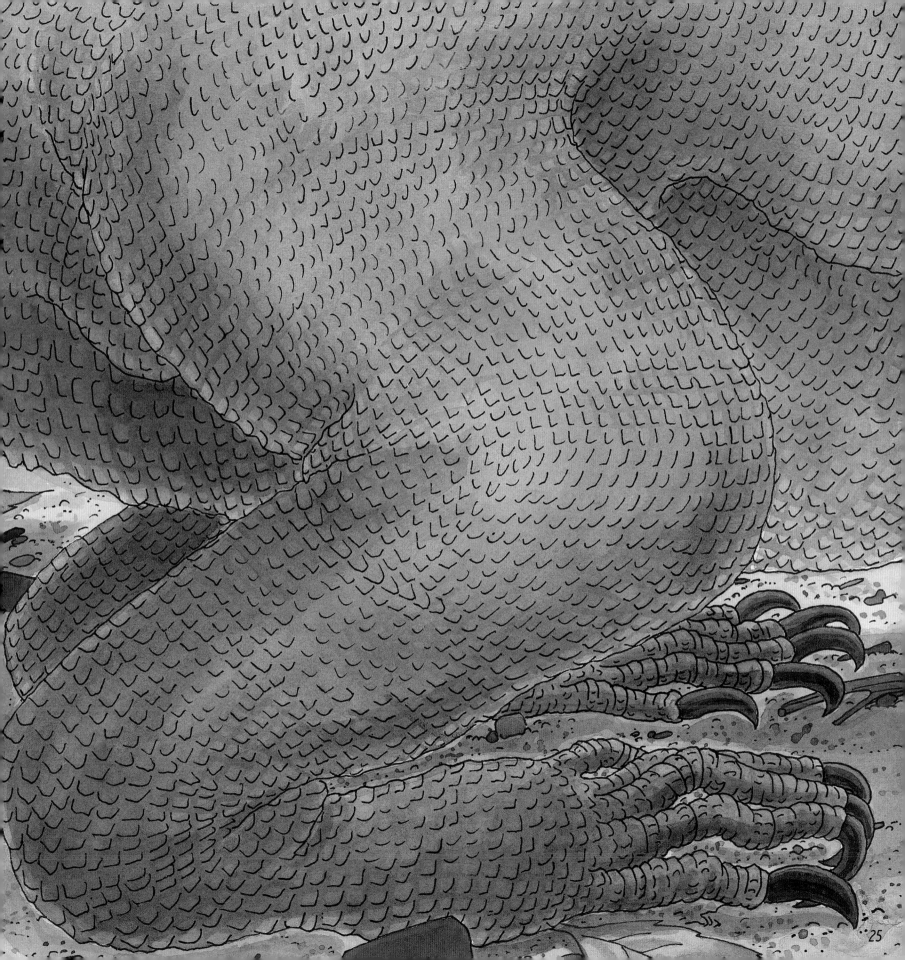

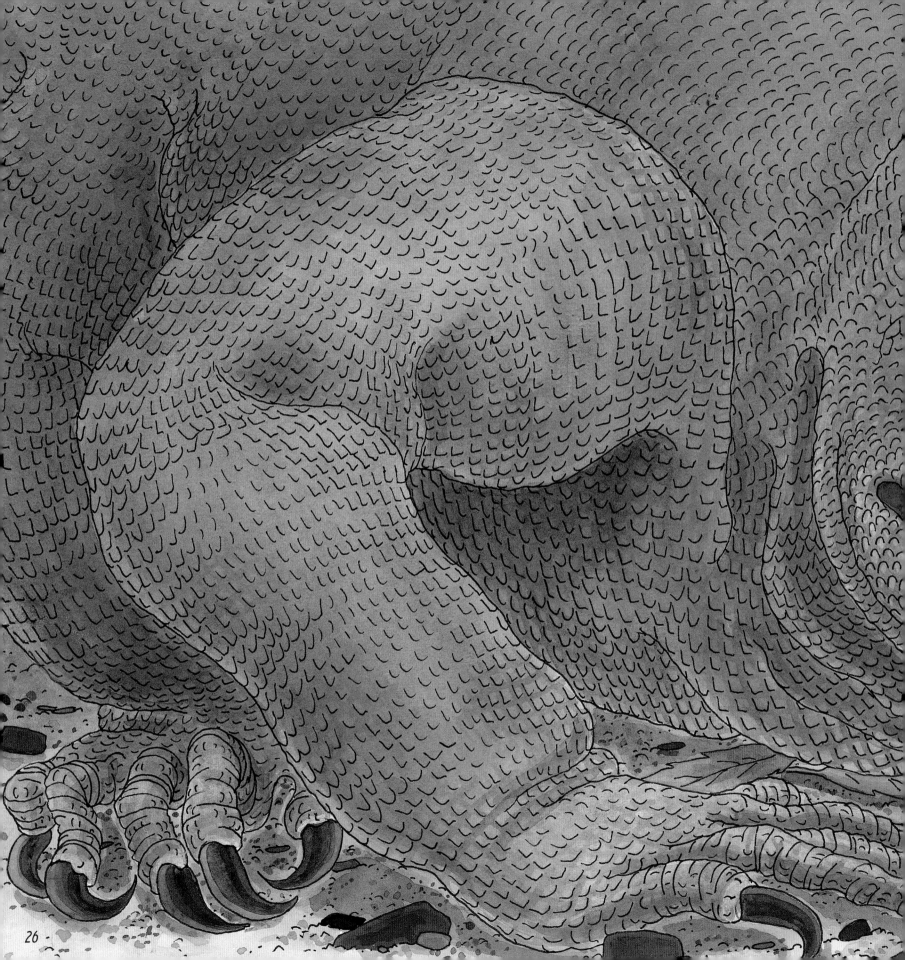

MORE ABOUT LIZARDS

Some skinks, like the FIVE-LINED SKINK (*Plestiodon fasciatus*), *hibernate* in cold weather beneath leaves, rocks, logs, or soil. They've been found as deep as 8 feet (about 2.4 meters) below the surface. Five-lined skinks are one of the most common lizards in the eastern United States. They can live in almost any *habitat* but prefer moist wooded areas with trees and rocks. One of the smaller lizards, they grow to 5 to 8.5 inches (13 to 21.5 centimeters) including their tail.

The ARMADILLO GIRDLED LIZARD (*Ouroborus cataphractus*) is small—from 3 to 8 inches (7.5 to 20 centimeters) excluding its tail. It prefers termites for dinner, but also eats other insects and spiders. It moves slowly and spends most of its time basking in the sun or hiding between rocks. It is found in South Africa and has been known to live up to 25 years in captivity.

The TEXAS HORNED LIZARD (*Phrynosoma cornutum*) is one of the largest of the fourteen species of horned lizards found in western North America. Horned lizards vary in length from 3 to 5 inches (7.5 to 12.5 centimeters). They eat mostly ants, but also termites, beetles, and grasshoppers. Though they are sometimes called 'horned toads,' they are not related to toads, which are amphibians, not reptiles.

GREEN ANOLES (*Anolis carolinensis*) coexist nicely with humans and are often seen on fences, plants, and windows. They are about 5 to 8 inches (12 to 20 centimeters) long, including their tail. They are excellent climbers and can even climb on glass. Females lay a single egg or a pair of eggs at eight-day intervals in the summer in a rotten tree trunk, a pile of leaves, or damp soil. They've been seen rolling or pushing their eggs to find a better nest.

FRINGE-TOED LIZARDS (*Uma*) can grow up to 10 inches (25.4 centimeters) including their tail. They have several traits tailored to their sand-dwelling lifestyle. To prevent sand from getting in their mouth, their upper jaw overlaps the lower one. Their nostrils can close, they have ear flaps, and they have overlapping eyelids that stop sand from getting in their eyes.

SLOW WORM

LEAF-TAILED GECKOS (*Uroplatus phantasticus*) are also called satanic leaf-tailed geckos. This species is small—only about 3.5 inches (9 centimeters) long including its tail. They're *nocturnal*, with large, marbled eyes, and are found in Madagascar, a big island off the east coast of Africa.

SANDFISH SKINKS (*Scincus scincus*) live in the Sahara and Arabian Deserts. They detect vibrations from nearby insects, like crickets and mealworms, and have them for dinner, so they're *insectivores* (which is a type of carnivore). They can grow up to 8 inches (about 20 centimeters) long, including the tail. This species is solitary—they don't hang out in colonies or groups.

GOLD-DUST DAY GECKOS (*Phelsuma laticauda*) are small—about 4 to 5.5 inches (10 to 14 centimeters). Like skinks, geckos can "release" their tails if attacked. The dropped tail gyrates for a few minutes, even when it's off, tricking the predator into thinking it's the gecko, who has escaped. Geckos like to eat insects and smaller lizards, as well as fruit and pollen and nectar from flowers.

LEOPARD GECKOS (*Eublepharis macularius*) are 7 to 11 inches long (18 to 28 centimeters) including their tail. They eat insects such as cockroaches, crickets, and grasshoppers, and worms. They store fat in their plump tails. This gecko is native to Asia and the Middle East, and lives in habitats such as rock deserts, grasslands, and low mountains.

The FLORIDA WORM LIZARD (*Rhineura floridana*) is not always considered to be a true lizard. It is 7 to 11 inches in length (18 to 28 centimeters), although other kinds of worm lizards, which are found on most continents, can grow up to 30 inches (76 centimeters) long. It has no ears and can't see well because it has recessed rudimentary eyes covered in skin and scales.

The JACKSON'S CHAMELEON (*Trioceros jacksonii*) lives in woodlands and forests, mainly in Kenya and Tanzania in Africa. Including its tail, it's usually 6 to 10 inches (15 to 25 centimeters) long, but it can grow to 15 inches (38 centimeters) long. The males sometimes have jousting battles with one another using their special horns.

The THORNY DEVIL (*Moloch horridus*) is also called a "thorny dragon." It is small and covered with spikes. It grows up to 8.3 inches long (21 centimeters) including its tail, and can live as long as fifteen to twenty years. Devils can change color to match their surroundings, usually staying grey, red, and orange or yellow.

The PARACHUTE GECKO (*Ptychozoon*) lives in Southeast Asia. Its brown-and-tan-patterned coloring acts as camouflage in the forest, helping it blend in with bark and tree limbs. These flying geckos can grow to be 6 to 8 inches (15 to 20 centimeters) long.

The COMMON COLLARED LIZARD (*Crotaphytus collaris*) grows up to 8 to 15 inches (20 to 38 centimeters) in total length, including the tail. It has a large head, powerful jaws, and long, strong hind legs. Its average life span is between five to eight years. It's the state reptile of Oklahoma, where it is called the "Mountain boomer."

VEILED CHAMELEON (*Chamaeleo calyptratus*) adults range from 14 to 24 inches (35 to 61 centimeters) including their tail. They are *arboreal* (tree-dwelling) and in the wild live mainly in Yemen and Saudi Arabia, but they are also kept as pets.

TOKAY GECKOS (*Gekko gecko*) are large for a gecko. Males average 13 to 16 inches (33 to 40 centimeters) long and females about 8 to 12 inches (20 to 30 centimeters). They are arboreal and spend a lot of time climbing high up on trees and resting on cliffs in rainforests and moist, rocky areas in south and southeast Asia, including on many islands.

A GREEN PLUMED BASILISK (*Basiliscus plumifrons*) can grow up to 3 feet long (almost 1 meter), including its tail. It is a member of the iguana family and is found in Central America, living in rainforests, close to a body of water. Because it can "walk on water" to escape predators and find food, some call this basilisk the "Jesus Christ lizard." Their diet includes insects, spiders, snails, crawfish, smaller lizards, and even small mammals.

GILA MONSTERS (*Heloderma suspectum*) live in the southwest United States and in Mexico in deserts, canyons, and woodlands. They are the largest lizard in the United States. Including their tail, they can grow up to 22 inches (56 centimeters) long. The Gila monster is a "beaded" lizard. The markings are different on every individual.

FRILLED LIZARDS (*Chlamydosaurus kingii*) are big—almost 3 feet (91 centimeters) long, including their tail. Like many lizards, frill-necked lizards are carnivores. Besides butterflies, they like feeding on ants, cicadas, beetles, and termites. Though insects are their primary source of food, they also consume spiders, mice, and sometimes other lizards. Females lay one or two *clutches* of 6 to 25 soft-shelled eggs a year, with a 2- to 3-month incubation period before they hatch.

GREEN IGUANAS (*Iguana iguana*) live in Central and South America and have become an invasive species in Florida, California, Texas, and Hawaii. In cold weather, they sometimes go into a stuper and fall out of trees. They are really big—adult sizes range from about 4 feet (1.2 meters) to 6.6 feet (2 meters). Iguanas can live up to twenty years in captivity.

The KOMODO DRAGON (*Varanus komodoensis*) is the largest member of the monitor family, a type of big lizard with a long neck, powerful tail and claws, and well-developed limbs. Females lay up to thirty eggs, which take nine months to incubate. Baby Komodo dragons are vulnerable to cannibalism by adults, so the juveniles spend the beginning of their lives living in trees. Their claws make them excellent climbers, but only when they're young. As adults, they become too heavy to climb trees.

AUTHOR'S NOTE

My interest in lizards started when I did a book on deserts a few years ago. As you have read in this book, there are many kinds of lizards living in deserts. Then I did a book on the rainforest. More lizards. My books on birds, bugs, rodents, and snakes involve lizards, as either predators or prey.

Lizards live all over the world. They've been around for hundreds of millions of years, long before humans came along, and in all sizes and shapes and colors, with lots of different behaviors. But now lizards in many of Earth's ecosystems are being threatened. Certain species have had to move to higher, cooler altitudes to survive global warming. Others are losing their homes as wetlands dry up or become polluted and forests are burned or cut down. Some are hunted by humans for their skin or captured as pets.

As we've seen in this book, there are many harmless, unique, and even beautiful lizards— we should care about these fascinating creatures. Please help preserve their homes. They just want to live their lives, like you and me.

EMERALD SWIFT

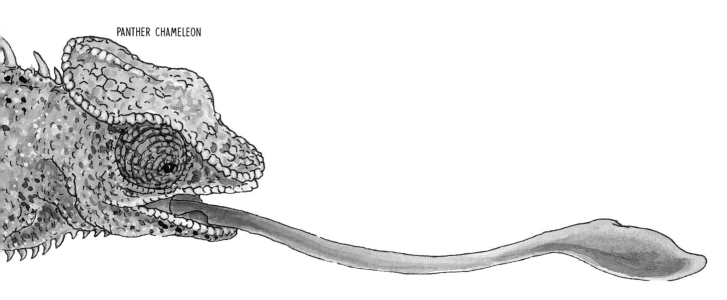

PANTHER CHAMELEON

BOOKS

Badger, David. *Lizards*. Stillwater, MN: Voyageur Press, 2002.

Greer, Allen E., Editor. *Reptiles*. Australia: Time-Life Books, 1996

Hoena, Blake. *Everything Reptiles*. Washington, DC: National Geographic Kids, 2016

Hughes, Catherine D. *Little Kids First Big Book of Reptiles and Amphibians*. Washington, DC: National Geographic Kids, 2020

McCarthy, Colin. *DK Eyewitness: Reptile*. New York: DK/Penguin Random House, 2012.

Sax, Boria. *Lizard*. London, UK: Reaktion Books Ltd, 2017

WEBSITES

Smithsonian: https://nationalzoo.si.edu/animals/exhibits/reptile-discovery-center

San Diego Zoo: https://animals.sandiegozoo.org/animals/lizard

The Reptile Database: http://reptile-database.reptarium.cz/

Elsevier, Science Direct: https://www.sciencedirect.com/topics/immunology-and-microbiology/lizard

World Wildlife Fund: https://www.worldwildlife.org/

National Geographic Kids: https://kids.nationalgeographic.com/animals/reptiles

GLOSSARY

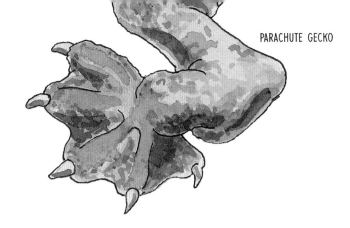

PARACHUTE GECKO

arboreal: lives in a tree

appendage: a part of an animal projecting from the main body and typically smaller with a distinct shape or function

bipedal: when an animal uses two legs for walking

camouflage: when an animal uses patterns, shapes, or colors that help it blend into its surroundings and hide from predators or prey

carnivore: an animal that eats other animals

cartilage: a tough, flexible tissue that sometimes connects bones to muscles (human noses and ears are made of cartilage)

clutch: a group of eggs laid by some female animals, such as birds or reptiles

cold-blooded: an animal whose temperature changes with its surroundings instead of being regulated internally

dewlap: a fold or pouch of loose skin under a creature's chin or throat

habitat: the natural home of an animal, such as forests, parks, deserts, or wetlands

hibernate: when an animal remains inactive during cold months, often in a burrow or cave

insectivore: a plant or animal that eats insects

membrane: a soft, thin, flexible sheet or layer

metabolism: chemical processes that occur inside an animal to maintain life, like burning food to create energy or warmth

nocturnal: active at night and asleep during the day

polyphyodont: an animal whose teeth are constantly replaced, including crocodiles, many toothed fish, and even elephants

predator: a creature that hunts other animals for food

species: a group of individuals with common attributes that can reproduce with each other

venom: chemicals that an animal uses to kill or paralyze prey, usually delivered by a sting or bite

AUSTRALIAN SHINGLEBACK LIZARD

INDEX

CHAMELEON

Page numbers in italic type refer to illustrations.

anole
  green 5, *5*

amphibians (differences from reptiles) 3

armadillo girdled lizard 4, *4*, 28

Australian shingleback lizard *30*

basilisk
  green-plumed 16, *16-17*, 29

camouflage 7, 11, 14, 28

chameleon *32*
  Jackson's 10, *10*, 28
  nano-chameleon 3
  panther *30*
  veiled 14, *14*, 29

collared lizard *1*, 13, *13*, 29

color changing 5, 14

cold-blooded 3

defenses against predators 3, 4, 5, 6, 11, 13, 18, 28, 29

diet 3, 8, 10, 11, 14, 16, 18, 20, 22, 28, 29

ears 3, 28

eggs *2*, 3, 4, 8, 28, 29

emerald swift 29

eyes 3, 5, 7, 8, 9, 14, 28, 29

feet 6, 7, 8, 9, 12, 14, 15, 16, *29*, *31*, *32*

fence lizard 2

fringe-toed lizards 6, *6*, 28

frilled lizard
  Australian 18, *18-19*, 29

gecko 3
  gold-dust day 8, *8*, 28
  leaf-tailed *3*, 7, *7*, 28
  leopard 9, *9*, 28
  parachute 12, *12*, 29
  tokay 15, *15*, 29

Gila monster 3, 20, *20-21*, 29

habitats 3, 6, 7, 8, 11, 13, 14, 16, 22, 24, 28, 29

hibernation 28

iguanas 3, 29
  green 22, *22-23*, 29

jaw 4, 7, 15, 18, 20, 28, 29

Komodo dragon 3, 24, *24-27*, 29, *32*

legs 6, 8, 9, 12, 13, 16, 18, 22, 29, 31

lifespan 28, 29

Madagascar day lizard *3*

Mexican beaded lizards 3

monitors 3

mouths 3, 7, 15, 16, 18, 24, 28, 29

noses 7, 18, 28, 31

predator 3, 4, 5, 6, 11, 18, 22, 24, 28, 29

reproduction 3, 4, 8, 28, 29

skink 3, 4
  five-lined 4, *4*, 28
  sandfish 7, *7*, 28

sizes 3, 24, 28-29

slow worm lizard *28*

sounds made 7, 15

speed 6, 13, 16

tails 3, 4, 7, 10, 11, 16, 20, 22, 28, 29, *30*, *31*

teeth 3, 9, 20, 31

Texas horned lizard 5, *5*, 28

thorny devil 11, *11*, 28

toes 6, 7, 8, 9, 14, 15

tongues 3, 8, 10, 24, *28*, *30*

venom 3, 20, 24, 31

worm lizard 3, 8, *8-9*, 28

KOMODO DRAGON